America
Rediscovered

America Rediscovered

Reuel F. Walker, Jr.

Library of Congress Catalog Card Number: 85-70295
ISBN: 0-9606984-1-8
ISBN: 0-9606984-2-6 (Deluxe)

This book
is dedicated to a group called
"THE SILENT AMERICANS"

definition: THE SILENT AMERICANS:

These are those Americans that support the Constitution of the United States, are willing to work for a living, take pride in their accomplishments, have moral character, respect the laws of the land and are not selective about the ones that they obey, are willing to fight and die for their country if a true threat was in evidence, believe in the young people that challenge their peers and grow up into the future leaders of our society, and possess a strong belief in God unto which they will some day have to atone. These positive thinking people believe in themselves and the future of the World. This group described is normally called the Majority within the United States of America. They make very little noise until someone violates their freedom or threatens their way of life.

Acknowledgements

There have been so many wonderful people that have provided words of encouragement throughout the development of this project, I really don't know where to begin with my thanks. The Park, Recreation, and Tourism Departments of the various states that so willingly contributed their time and materials. The representatives of the National Park Service that freely gave us their input on where to locate scenic vistas and wild animal overlooks. The hundreds of people we met in our travels, who shared their favorite places with us. Especially the lady from Massachusetts that we met on the ferry from Alaska, that told us that she had never encountered anyone that had the appreciation for the country that we had.

We would also thank the various corporations, businesses, and business acquaintances that contributed time, services, products, and other signs of encouragement. Only with cooperation from this group, would this venture have been possible.

Contents

Introduction

Basically, I have always considered myself to be a stable individual. For twenty four years, I worked at the same position, with about all the security I could use. Raised two children through high school and college, paid for a home, and did most everything that the book says a man should accomplish for happiness. Even with all this, I still felt the need to satisfy a recurring itch.

In December 1983, I decided to scratch my itch so I left my secure position and decided to travel around the United States. Most people would have been content with the trip, but not me. I wanted to tell everyone my impressions about the things I observed, and the wonders to behold. It was probably the desire to share my world with others less fortunate that prompted me to undertake this book. With this in mind, let me explain my thinking process regarding the adventure.

Being a Professional Photographer I felt that I would be able to show the world the things I observed. Then to keep track of the sequence of travels, a journal of the trip and the people we met was a necessity. This is how we were able to recall facts, dates and people that we felt had something to contribute to the story.

We picked up a motorhome in January 1984, and started out on our odyssey around the country. During the course of the next twelve months, we were to visit all fifty states in all seasons of the year. In order to accomplish this feat, we would travel over 85,000 miles by car, motorhome and airplane. We also encountered weather from 113 degrees in Texas during May to snow in June during the trip driving to Alaska. We took a total of over 30,000 pictures and felt we had only scratched the surface of what there is to see.

The sights to behold in this country are too numerous to mention. The only thing I can say is that there is something for everyone out there. From a baby bird found in a Saguaro cactus nest to the magnificent grizzly in the wilds of Alaska, there is more wildlife than even I had imagined. The majestic bald eagle, the nation's symbol, flying freely in Seward, Alaska is a sight that everyone should see in their lifetime. It is also amazing to see the deserts, where it looks as though nothing could survive, and to walk in close and see the cactus in full bloom. The fall colors in Michigan and New England are also a sight to behold. To see the epitome of man's abilities as shown in the space shuttle lift off from a Florida beach.

When you go on a trip such as we experienced, be sure to get off the Interstate Highway System and see the little towns and meet the people. The little restaurants that you try offer a variety of local dishes that will make you cry for more. As you travel around the country through this book, be aware that we try to notice the little things as well as the monuments. Don't travel the countryside without seeing it.

The most important asset that this country has are its people. We met the most friendly people on this trip that we have ever met. Probably the key to making new friends is the ability to accept them as they are without offending them by telling them they need to change this or that. By talking and listening to bellhops, retired executives, farmers, millionaires, and the many hundreds of others we met, we were able to literally take the pulse of the majority of the people we talked to.

During the entire trip, we have asked the people we met the same question. It was phrased, "If you had a visitor to this country from Europe, what would you show them in your state for them to remember and take home?" From all of these people, we were given names of places in the country with natural beauty. Not a single person suggested taking their visitors to New York City, Atlanta, Los Angeles, or Seattle. All large metropolitan areas have about the same good and bad points.

Now that we have briefly taken you through the intent of the book, we hope you enjoy the rest of your journey. Look at the pictures as if you had been there, and let your mind imagine our feelings. We feel that this country is one to be extremely proud of and we feel that the people we met felt the same way. Try to understand that this book is something that I felt I had to do, because with my strong feelings about this country, no one else could have put as much of their heart into it.

Observations of Life in the U.S.A.

Traveling around the United States collecting data and photographs for a book, we found that there were many people who wanted to say something positive about this country. In order to remember the statements and be able to recall accurately, we maintained a journal of our travels and conversations with these people. So that we will not embarrass these new friends, we have elected to paraphrase and combine statements to, hopefully, properly convey their thoughts.

The statements that were made to me represent a feeling I had before this journey was undertaken. I am proud to have met all of the people that have confirmed my belief in this country and its people. There are many nations, and groups within our own country, that criticize and throw verbal stones regarding our democratic system of living our lives. With the strength that I have discovered within our people, the U.S.A. will survive and rise to lead other nations by example to a secure and richer enjoyment of life.

Reading and thinking these statements through, I hope that you will be able to recognize the greatness of this country and what it stands for. It has taken us over 200 years to accomplish this much. What can you or your heirs contribute to improve the quality of life we presently enjoy?

Teenagers

Teenagers are probably the most misunderstood and underrated class of citizens in our country. We as parents have disappointed them in various ways. They have been condemned as a class, due to the actions of a few. What was mischief thirty years ago, when we were their age, is serious trouble now. What confusion it must be to them.

Within our present crop of young people are the scientists, doctors, engineers, artists, writers and all of the other trades needed to make this great country excel and remain invincible to all. They are the leaders that will pick up where the senior citizens have taken us, and project us even further than we can presently imagine.

We, their parents, have laid the heaviest burden on our children. During the 60s and 70s, we underwent a period of internal dissention over a war that we apparently did not intend to win. Heroes were in short supply at this time. Also, during this same period, an inflationary spiral set in that required longer hours, multiple jobs, and less time at home. The family unit began to break down. Morality began to slide and many families could only adjust by divorce. All of the cases amounted to less guidance and attention for the children. This led to substitute peers, which did not have the mental maturity or experience to properly advise. We have always had immoral opportunists that prey on the disoriented and advised alcohol or narcotics for relief. Many young people fell victim to these temporary solutions, but the problem was only worse, when and if, they came out of it. The children have always been the victim. Many children only wanted their parents to pay attention, listen, and properly advise. Enough said?

The world will live through the hard times and land on its feet. Traveling around the country, my faith was reaffirmed in our young people. There are many "straight" young people ready to assume their places in society and also as the leaders of their generation. In Petoskey, Michigan and at a Tourist Information Office in Iowa there are at least two young people that will someday rise above the rest to lead.

Senior Citizens

How many times have we heard people put down senior citizens with terms like "senile," "out of step" and "simply not in the know"? Well nothing could be further from the truth. What is probably more accurate is that many were "turned out to pasture" by retirement, even when they were still productive.

Reflect on this if you would. This "over the hill gang" gave us most of the medical achievements during the past 40 years. They gave us many of the technological advances, including our first ventures into space. They were our teachers and taught us to excel in our own fields. They were our parents and guardians that taught us right from wrong. Many fought in wars overseas to protect our way of life. In general, they are the previous generation of young people that knew nothing, but got the job done anyway.

These people have many talents that we should acquire before it's too late. How many young people do you know that can repair a watch, tailor a suit, embroider a tablecloth, or cook an old-fashioned lemon meringue pie. Basically, these are becoming lost arts.

These people deserve and should receive social security, welfare assistance and medicare without threat of cuts. These people have "paid their dues" and in their golden years deserve their just rewards. They also need to be challenged to keep their minds alert and agile. If they stay in touch with the family they have raised, the grandchildren can provide the challenge and learn the dying arts before it's too late. Leave the rest homes for the truly senile and infirmed that cannot provide for themselves.

Leadership

American business and industry are apparently falling behind in the race to provide effective leadership capabilities within their respective fields. For years, it was common for the world to think of American industry as the leaders in management. America, several years ago, began to go for any "fad like" management styles that would give them more production for the same or less dollars per unit of production. We seem to have strayed away from the theory of a job to be done the absolute best that is possible.

We fell into the old time "sweat shop" approach to work. If a business pushes its workers for increased production, the worker will quickly lose interest in any goal except keeping his job. Once you have killed a man's initiative, you find his creative powers will slide to the subconscious for fear of losing his security.

After you have killed a worker's initiative, he works hard to meet the guidelines set up as his production goal. The possibility of errors creep into the product. What better way to cut product cost than to cut back or eliminate quality control. This is a false economy since one defective product can eliminate a company from a competitive position. Is this logical leadership?

The America leadership corp had entirely too many weak leaders that have let their egos rule over common sense and logic. To make the situation even more severe, these "leaders" have surrounded themselves with equally weak subordinates. In order to maintain control without making a positive decision, management begins to play games with employee's lives. Where this may work with some, the more intelligent type will not knowingly participate in games. The more emotionally mature employee then loses faith in the ability of top management. This weakens the entire top management of a productive team. Many retired people felt they represented a potential threat to management.

We are not intimating that all corporations are run by ineffective or weak leaders. There are many large, aggressive corporations that are run by the strongest of leaders. These leaders hire and utilize their workers to the full potential. By full utilization of the employees, they stimulate their creative abilities and usually this results in extra effort. For their efforts, the employees are rewarded for their achievements. This reward usually comes in the form of a "thank you" or a simple pat on the back. This represents recognition of a job well done. This is the way you draw the best out of people. Using logic and common sense, you get maximum effort from your people and combined with your leadership, how can the idea fail?

Education

One of the strong points about the United States of America has been its fine educational system. A look at the literary, mathematical and scientific achievements show the results of our system.

During our travels, we found many people along the way that expressed concern regarding the state of our educational system. One factor that contributed to the decision to develop this book is the apparent lack of emphasis on Geography. We discovered many young people that did not know what state various major cities were located in. Other questions of a geographic nature brought looks of amazement to their faces. Do not at this point condemn the young people, we let it happen.

Back in the 60s and 70s, the United States was in a transition period and everyone's conscience was trying to straighten out past wrongs. Acting in haste, as we frequently do, we made some errors in judgment. These errors can always be seen in hindsight.

Where we made our error on integration was to integrate all grades at one time. When deficiencies showed up in minorities, the Government set percentages of which races were to be passed. This resulted in standards being lowered to permit more young people to pass.

Now we need to raise the standards of education back to higher levels. With more tools, such as calculators and computers, the young people are prepared for more challenge. Also, we could develop two high school curriculums; college preparatory and general development.

In some way, we need to impress on teachers of the very young of their position as a role model. Children are very observant and try hard to present the image they think their role models want to see.

When you think of your good times in school, chances are you will recall one particular class that was your favorite. This class is always the one in which the teachers took an active interest in their students. These teachers always showed up at after school events to cheer on their students. The teacher has to develop a relationship that lets the students know that they are their friend and interested in their concerns. This will stimulate the students desire to want to come to school and look forward to the challenge.

Prejudice

While on Molokai Island in Hawaii, I made an observation that is worth repeating. I commented that "I see that apparently there is no prejudice or animosity here in Hawaii." The big native told me, "Brother, we have so many ethnic and cultural groups in our blood, we really don't know who to hate." What a problem, they don't know who to hate! He was asked if he would like to come to the mainland and give some lessons.

In reality, aren't we on the mainland made up of just as diverse backgrounds? Then why are there such strong feelings present about ethnic groups and minorities within this country? Are there valid reasons why these feelings are present?

As we all know, all people including the minorities are free to enjoy most of their ethnic, cultural, or religious practices as they wish. Some of these differences appear strange to an outsider, but as we learn more about them, we can understand their meaning. Perhaps if we took more interest in others, we would understand each other better. Sometimes we get all wrapped up in our own priorities and tend to forget about others.

Probably the biggest source of irritation occurs when a minority group tries to force their practices or beliefs off on the majority. This can occur when a minority lobby group succeeds in getting the Congress to consider or pass a bill that will aid only their society. In doing this, it can work a hardship and/or expense on the majority. We all tend to resent something being forced on us.

When your automobile is broken, you don't request that a white repairman fix it. You want it repaired regardless of the color of a man's skin as long as he is qualified. When you watch television for entertainment, you don't turn the dial if they have Mexican talent. If you are in the hospital and require a specialist, you could care less if the specialist is Oriental. The key to all this is that you want someone that is qualified for the service you desire.

The way to eliminate prejudice is to judge each person on their own merit. Do not pre-judge an individual by the color of their skin, the cut of their hair, or the way they talk. Being from the South, several people along the way have said I talk funny. The fact is that I felt they had an accent, but I didn't want to mention it.

Patriotism

Driving around the country, we saw American Flags flying proudly from flagpoles at farms, fast food establishments, new car dealerships, and motorhomes. We saw American Flags painted on mailboxes, silos, water tanks, and buildings. Throughout this land, there is evidence of a definite pride in the American Flag and all it represents.

Webster's New Collegiate Dictionary defines patriotism as "love of country, devotion to the welfare of one's country." They neglected to include the tears in your eyes when the flag goes by in a parade, or a band plays the Star Spangled Banner. They also forgot to mention the pride and tears when "our side" wins a gold medal. All of these things say Patriotism or pride in one's country.

America has for many years been known as the "melting pot" to the immigrants that selected the United States as their new homeland. By moving to this country, they learned our ways, our language, and our laws to become better American citizens. Isn't it a shame when immigrants come to this country and want us to adopt their ways and language. If they wanted to come to the United States because it appeared better than the quality of life they had at home, why shouldn't they adapt to our way of living, American style?

Rather than use guns, violence, and suffering to bring about changes in government, we in the United States prefer the ballot box. In this manner, the basis of our democracy prevails and the majority vote selects the candidate preferred by the people. This brings about peaceful changes that affect over 226 million people. Is there a better way?

America
Rediscovered

Mid-Atlantic Area

Here in the middle area of the East Coast, we find the hub of activity for the financial, judicial, and legislative world that affects the remainder of the United States. From Washington, D.C. to New York City, the majority of the population is centered and all of the assets and detriments of big city life are concentrated. Many of the more outstanding museums, art galleries, and educational institutions are located in this area. Let's look at some of the areas a little closer.

Starting with Washington, D.C., we find the center of the executive and legislative branches of the government. The Capitol Building with all of its splendor houses the meeting halls for the House of Representatives and the Senate on either end. The Congressional Offices are located nearby for easy access. At the far end of the Mall, we find the Washington Monument that pays homage to an American patriot and past President. On either side of the grassy mall between these two structures, we find other impressive structures such as the Supreme Court, the National Gallery of Art, and the Smithsonian Institution. In these buildings, we find the high court of the land, national art treasures, and the inventions that help build America. One thing that you immediately notice when you first view this area is the architecture of the buildings. The early planners of this country in laying out and developing Washington, definitely wanted it to be a showplace. They were successful in their efforts.

Working our way up the coast, we next come to the historic state of Maryland. The State House in Annapolis has been in continuous use since 1772 and would be well worth the effort, if you can get by to see it. Another sight to see would be the row houses with their marble steps in Baltimore. The restored waterfront area has helped tremendously in the downtown revitalization effort. Getting away from Baltimore, the Harpers Ferry area while historically important is also a beautiful spot to visit. At the Harpers Ferry National Park, you can relive the raid on the U.S. Armory that eventually cost John Brown his life.

In Delaware, one of the prettiest spots is along the coast near Rehoboth Beach on the Atlantic Ocean. While I was talking with two fishermen in down coats, we observed a young lady in swimming. Anything is possible in this country. Another beautiful sight is the twin bridges near Wilmington that carry you to New Jersey. If you happen to travel the bridges at night, the DuPont plant with all of its lights is very impressive.

As you drive through Delaware, you will pass close to another attraction, Winterthur, that certainly deserves a stop. This is the former home of H.E. duPont who inherited the estate in 1927. This estate houses one of the most astounding collections of antiques that you have seen displayed, in a most unusual manner. Where most people collect an item to bring into their home, Mr. duPont collected entire rooms complete with all furnishings. The house has grown over the years to its present gigantic proportions. In keeping with the buildings, the grounds are tastefully landscaped to show a different picture during every season.

New Jersey is a state of extreme contrasts. From the peaceful section of coastline with the fishing crowd to the built up areas around the industrial facilities, this transition can take place in a few short miles. Only a short drive from the fabulous beaches and casinos at Atlantic City, you can find the quaint Historic Village of Smithville. Here we found a step back in time to the period of fishing vessels and shops that resemble the construction of the period. The Quail Hill and Smithville restaurants are popular even off season.

In the Cape May area, you will still find the ferry service to Delaware and the South. The Cape May area is also popular with the surf fishermen trying to snag the elusive Blues. The commercial fishers use this harbor to fish the Mid-Atlantic seas.

Crossing the state line, we come to the Brandywine Valley of Pennsylvania. This area includes the Chester and Delaware counties of the state and is part of the residential area for Philadelphia. Also in this area are some of the most spectacular museums and gardens in this area of the country. The Brandywine River Museum at Chadd's Ford is housed in an old grist mill that has been converted into one of the most modern art museums that was visited. This museum is home to an outstanding collection of paintings by the Wyeth family and to many other artists famous for their achievements.

Just down the road, we find Longwood Gardens with its 350 acres of outdoor gardens and the glassed conservatories. The conservatorium houses about 20 indoor gardens displayed in a most pleasing fashion. Their brochure boasts of their having 14,000 different varieties of plants, and there is no doubt in my mind that they did not exaggerate this number. Another great feature about this attraction, is that they are open twelve months of the year and host over 200 performing art events a year. Truly an outstanding place to spend the day.

One area of this state that is truly worth mentioning is the Amish country near Intercourse. The Amish are the most Conservative order of the Mennonite religion and have their origin in Europe. In this area, you have a living example of the right to practice your own beliefs without interference from your fellow man. The Amish were the first to practice the separation of church and state back in Europe. Even now, they practice nonconformity and feel that some trends of progress lead to the break down of the family unit. For this reason, they will still be found driving horse and buggies rather than an automobile. Other examples of their beliefs are evident when you visit the area.

In Philadelphia, we find many scenic places to visit. Independence Hall is where the Constitution of the United States of America was drawn up and signed by our forefathers. These men had so much vision and belief in our country that very few changes have been necessary to this Constitutional document in over two centuries. On display in the same area is the Liberty Bell, which developed a crack while tolling the death of Chief Justice Marshall.

New York City serves with its Wall Street as the financial center for the United States. With a population of 9,119,737 people in the metropolitan area, New York City is one of the most densely populated cities in the world. This converts to 23,494 people per square mile. With its tall buildings and other impressive sights, it is truly a remarkable place.

Upstate from the big city, we find the resort town of Lake Placid in the Adirondack mountains. It was here in 1980 that the Winter Olympics were held and the hockey team made their mark in the history books. Even now, we can still see the impressive ski jump facilities and the current Olympic hopefuls' training facilities. Close by, but still in the Lake Placid area is the homesite and grave of American patriot, John Brown. Now a State Park kept up by the state, the old home, out buildings, and farm are well worth the visit. A lot of history can be learned by visiting the historic sites found throughout this country.

Across the state in the Northwest corner, you can visit one of the more spectacular sights that occurs in nature. Niagara Falls is composed of two separate falls, Horseshoe Falls and the American Falls. The American Falls are on the New York State side and the Horseshoe Falls join the United States and Canada. Rainbow Bridge is the common crossing point for a quick trip to Canada. The State of New York has developed a great park around the approaching rivers to the falls.

This entire area was visited during the off season and was practically deserted. Many of the tourist attractions were closed, but we were not trying to photograph them, so it really didn't matter. The people we met were those living in the area year round and proud to be helpful.

Washington, D.C.

Spring flowers brighten the Capital.

The Botanical Gardens are popular in the spring.

The Museum of Natural History is host to many traveling exhibits.

5

The Washington Monument is framed by the fabled Japanese Cherry Blossoms.

The National Gallery of Art contains many unique paintings and sculptures.

Maryland

The fog begins to settle on a coastal harbor.

Dockmasters shed guards the pier.

Typical Maryland seacoast scene.

Surf fishing along the Maryland Coast is a popular past time.

Fishing boats frequently tie up on inland rivers such as this one at Federalsburg.

9

Delaware

Front view of Winterthur.

Rear view of Winterthur gives you some idea of the size.

Flaming Maple at Winterthur.

Gate and bench at Winterthur.

Pennsylvania

Front view Brandywine River Museum.

Side view showing new addition to Brandywine River Museum.

Right. *View of display area in Brandywine River Museum.*

Below. *Display area with Wythe Paintings.*

Longwood Gardens Conservatory.

Interior view, Longwood Gardens.

14

A child enjoys one of the many Animal Topiaries in the Conservatory at Longwood Gardens.

There is a room full of many different species of Orchids in the Conservatory.

A Camel Topiary enjoys the crowd.

15

There are many varieties of Orchids at Longwood.

16

Amish farmer with four horse cultivator.

Amish farmer with horse drawn rake.

New Jersey

Popular shops at the Towne of Historic Smithville.

Display at Quail Hill Restaurant at Historic Smithville.

Surf fisherman brave the chilly breezes in search of Blues.

Fishing boat leaving the harbor at Cape May.

19

Scene of marsh along the Atlantic Coast.

Ferry leaving Cape May for Lewes, Delaware.

New York

Scenic church at Lake Placid.

Olympic Ski Jumps at Lake Placid.

American Falls with Horseshoe Falls in the background at Niagara Falls.

22

Confederate Memorial at Niagara Falls Park.

Popcorn Stand at Niagara Falls Park.

John Brown's family home at Lake Placid.

The New England Area

As we look at the New England Area, we find six states that have a strong resemblance to each other in geographical features. Most of them have some amount of coastline and various types of harbors. There are mountainous areas in several states that have led to the development of winter sport facilities. This area has four distinct seasons although the temperature extremes are much lower than those found in the Southern states. To explain this more clearly, let's talk a little about each.

Heading North from New York State, we first come to Connecticut. One of the smallest states, it is also one of the more prosperous. Connecticut was settled in 1639, and granted statehood in 1788. To show how progressive this state was, it adopted the "Fundamental Orders" in 1639 which is considered to be the first state constitution. Presently, this state is the major manufacturer of ball and roller bearings, submarines, and helicopters.

Typical of the population along the East Coast, this area is keenly aware of their heritage and how they arrived at their present status. With approximately 253 miles of shoreline, the people of Connecticut are deeply interested in the sea. It should come as no surprise that Mystic Seaport has one of the finest living museums dedicated to the ways of the sea utilized in the development of this area. Perhaps one of the most exciting exhibits is the Charles W. Morgan, the last of the great wooden whaling vessels still afloat. At various times during the day, there are sail handling demonstrations on the C.W. Morgan, whale boat exercises, and many sea chants to be heard through out the area. The village has been recreated to depict the type of construction and businesses that you would have encountered during the turn of the century.

As you travel through Connecticut, you will also see the quaint villages that the people are so proud of. Almost every town has a square in which the heroes, past and present, are honored. Salisbury and Norfolk are two just such type of towns. From the white churches to the monuments, these towns are typical New England. In addition to seeing the sites, you will enjoy talking with the local people and comparing views on a variety of subjects. You will be able to see how their views differ from yours based on their point of view. You will also find that on basic ideas, their view is the same you would encounter all through this country.

In Massachusetts, you have a study in contrasts. From the busy metropolitan area of Boston to the serenity found on Cape Cod. With miles of beaches and wildlife refuges, there is plenty of room to unwind on the Cape. To make sure that the peaceful area on the cape is preserved for future generations, the United States Government has established the Cape Cod National Seashore Park which is for the enjoyment of all. Near North Eastham, you can view the Nauset Light which is an operating lighthouse. Perhaps one of the most spectacular things as you meander around the cape, is to discover the salt water marshes, the shore birds that inhabit these areas and, in general, to be able to view the peaceful existence of these people.

Moving on to Plymouth, we found ourselves in a historic area with many beautiful sights to see. In the middle of Historic Plymouth, you can find the Jenney Grist Mill. This Grist Mill is a 20th Century reconstruction of the first grist mill in the Pilgrim Colony. It operates continuously and is a close reproduction of the original 17th Century Mill.

As you wander around suburban Massachusetts, the scenery will surely capture your imagination. From autumn leaves laying on a stream to a foot print in the sand, Massachusetts surely has something for everyone.

Moving on to New Hampshire, we find an old established area that has many rememberances of the past still there for viewing. With their covered bridges, New Hampshire shows us the way that our forefathers navigated streams and rivers during foul weather. Around these covered bridges, you will find many recreational opportunities such as fishing and, in general, viewing the surroundings.

New Hampshire is perhaps more oriented to the outdoors than many other states that we have visited. There is a good deal of hiking and should you feel up to the challenge, you can hike in the area of Franconia Notch and see the Old Man of the Mountains. This rock outcrop that resembles a man's face is the New Hampshire State Emblem. In the same general area of New Hampshire, you can view the waterfalls that are located near Pinkum Notch. Both of these areas mentioned occur in a section of the state whose main geological feature is the White Mountains.

Adjacent to New Hampshire, we find one of the least populated states, Vermont. To make up for it's lack of population, we find one of the more scenic states with respect to natural beauty. Around Manchester, Vermont, you find many quaint, rustic motels that provide the very best in service. In addition, this area is oriented toward the family, and you even find specialty shops such as the Enchanted Doll House in which you will find toys for kids of all ages.

We hit Brattleboro during the fall of the year and were able to experience the fall colors, indian corn, and scarecrows for the children. Fall is great time for hayrides, walks through old corn fields and general enjoyment of the scenery. During this time of year, you can watch farmers preparing for the winter and readying their fields for the crops next spring.

Getting into Maine, we run into an area of the country with rocky shorelines, beautiful fall foliage and, in general, the peaceful contemplation of the oncoming winter. From the fog that causes sea and sky to blend together, to silent vigil of tools outside of a hardware store, all signs indicate that winter is coming. When we came to New Sharon, Maine, we ran into a service station operator that was extremely proud of his section of the state. He was helpful in directing us to a scenic photographic spot in which we were able to capture some of the fall foliage in all it's splendor. Other people were equally helpful in directing us around their area of the state of which they were extremely proud. It is with this enthusiasm that we encountered that we were able to capture on film many beautiful spots around the country in which the people themselves expressed pride in their particular section of the country.

Rhode Island is the smallest state, in area, which is part of these United States. What it lacks in size, its makes up for in cordial treatment for it's visitors. Basically a resort area, it has many beautiful homes, in which many of the people in larger cities take refuge during the warm summer months. By looking at the yachts and sailboats in the marinas, you can easily tell that the roots of Rhode Island are deeply tied to the sea itself.

To try and summarize the New England area, we think back about rocky coastlines, inland farm lands and majestic mountains. Perhaps the one thing that we have not mentioned is the warmth of the people. Basically, the people in this area pretty much mind their own business and, therefore, appear to an "outsider" to be somewhat of an introvert. Once accepted on their terms, they are some of the warmest, most concerned people we have met. Based on their history of colonial battles, the New England resident is deeply concerned about the future of the country. One only has to visit the area to realize their pride in what they have preserved from their patriotic and historical past.

Maine

The shore at Bailey's Island shows just how rugged and rocky the Maine Coast is.

The horizon is lost in a early morning fog at Bar Harbor.

Rowboats at rest create an interesting pattern at Camden.

The fall foliage brings beauty to everything at New Sharon.

The church at New Sharon stands tall in the fall foliage.

A brewing storm cannot squelch the sunlight near Phippsburg.

In Camden, boats are being readied for the oncoming winter.

A yard of antiques along Route 1 creates it's own beauty in Maine.

The fall comes early to Rock Ovens.

Even the roadside stations herald autumn.

The shovels and rakes stand tall in Wiscasset.

33

Vermont

Fall vegetables create a typical autumn scene near Putney.

Indian Corn is displayed for sale near Putney.

What's better for family fun than a hayride during the changing of the leaves.

A typical farm scene along Route 2 in Vermont.

Many attractive motels beckon the traveler in Vermont.

Toys for the kids of all ages are available at specialty shops.

36

New Hampshire

The last day of fishing season beckons to us all.

The great stone face has shone for many years.

OLD MAN
OF THE
MOUNTAINS
"THE GREAT STONE FACE"
48 FT FROM FOREHEAD TO CHIN
1200 FT. ABOVE PROFILE LAKE
3200 FT. ABOVE SEA LEVEL
FIRST SEEN BY WHITE MEN IN 1805.

THE NEW HAMPSHIRE STATE EMBLEM

The Old Man of the Mountains is the State Emblem for New Hampshire.

As we cross a covered bridge, the fall foliage is framed by it's beauty.

As we look at the covered bridge near Jackson, we can only marvel at the engineering genius.

Lower Left. *Many scenes in New Hampshire show us the beauty of the covered bridge.*

Lower right. *The fall leaves on a peaceful stream signal the oncoming winter.*

Massachusetts

In Plymouth, we find Jenney's Grist Mill still in operating condition.

Decorative windows displaying their wares await the traveler in Plymouth.

Sea grass protects our coast on Cape Cod.

We hope that all who visit our National Parks only leave footprints.

41

Nauset Light on Cape Cod still serves as a beacon for lost souls.

Peaceful scenes unfold as we ride along the highways on Cape Cod.

Connecticut

The Charles W. Morgan lies at anchor in Mystic
Seaport at Mystic, Connecticut.

Mystic Seaport contains all types of
sailing memorabilia of the New
England Heritage.

The Village at Mystic Seaport is typical of what you would have found in a seacoast town at the turn of the century.

Even the signs are reminiscent of maritime nostalgia.

The Mystic Seaport Village contained a number of businesses of the period.

44

Sailsbury, Connecticut is typical of a small New England Village.

In Norfolk, Connecticut the Town Square contains monuments to the past as well as churches of the present.

Even the churches have a certain majesty in Salisbury.

Rhode Island

The Trinity Church in Newport.

The homes in Newport feature a distinctive architectural appearance.

Boating is the chief tourist activity in Newport.

The American Flag flies proudly from many of the old homes.

Seagulls enjoying the surf.

The State Capitol is an impressive structure overlooking Providence.

Graves of Seafaring Men watch over the town of Newport.

The Southern States

For years, when people thought about the South they conjured up visions of Southern Belles, slow talking southern gentlemen, and horse and carriage to take the romantic couple off in the moonlight. Well, things have changed now, progress has come to the South and the Southerners with their knowledge and ability have been able to adapt well. According to the 1980 census, the South had approximately 23 per cent of the total U.S. population or 52,646,184 people. This population explosion has taken place on only 15 per cent of the total United States land area. Population in Florida alone has quadrupled in the last twenty years. With this tremendous increase in population has come the technology, the arts, and the ability to compete with other sections of the country on a worldwide basis. The days of taking advantage in negotiation of a slow talking Southerner are over. Southerners are not as inclined to act hastily without thinking things through. Just because a Southerner talks slow and has an accent, never underestimate them and consider them to be dumb or stupid. Some of the sharpest business men around make their home in the South.

A good portion of the South is covered with lush green vegetation, ample water supplies in the form of rivers and streams, and the necessary work force to make any project viable. With the high percentage of minorities, the South received a lot of unwarranted publicity 20 years ago when integration first became an issue. In reality, the South has accepted integration in a much smoother manner than we have read about in some of our neighboring areas. Rather than talk in generalities, lets look at the individual Southern States and determine what their assets and draw backs might be.

Virginia is called the home of Presidents. There have been more Presidents born in Virginia than any other state. As with other states along the eastern seaboard, Virginia offers a cross section of geographical terrain. From the coast with the beaches and the tidal flats, we go to rolling hills and in the western part of the state we have the Blue Ridge Mountains. Bounded on the East by the Atlantic Ocean and the Chesapeake Bay, commercial fishing plays a big part in to the economy of the state. In it's northern area, adjacent to Washington, D.C., government plays a large part in the economy.

General George Washington defeated Cornwallis at Yorktown in 1781, and Virginians played a big part in the establishment of the United States as a free and democratic nation. The Constitution of the United States was drawn up by Mr. Thomas Jefferson of Virginia, and subsequently ratified by the thirteen original colonies. Virginia, by it's central location and it's exposure to a wide variety of idiosyncrasies from people in other parts of the country, has always had a leadership role in the furnishing of qualified people to run this country.

One cannot think of North Carolina without thinking of tobacco and peanuts. Like Virginia, North Carolina enjoys a wide range in topographical features from the sandy beaches on the coast to the mountains in the western part of the state. Manufacturing, agriculture, and tobacco are the primary industries within the state. Textiles, Hi-tech, and the furniture industry in recent years have also contributed greatly to the economy.

When you have some delightful tourist attractions, such as Cape Hatteras on the shore and the Great Smoky Mountains to the west, North Carolina is indeed blessed with the natural beauty that invites tourism. When we think about Cape Hatteras, we cannot overlook the fact that the Wright Brothers pioneered in the development of the first sustained flight of a mechanical powered airplane at Kitty Hawk, North Carolina.

In the Wilmington area, we find many beautiful gardens that have been cultivated over the years for enjoyment of the visitors. One of the more spectacular of these gardens is located at Orton Plantation, which is approximately 15 miles south of Wilmington. The Orton Plantation was built around 1735 and is one of the more beautiful plantation homes available for viewing. While there, you can view the Chapel, the exterior of the main house and an old colonial cemetary. The old rice fields, which are directly in front of the house and flooded by the Cape Fear River, are presently used by the North Carolina Resources Commission as a Wildfowl Refuge. It is possible to view Great Blue Herons and other shore birds if you observe carefully.

Also in the Wilmington area, you find the U.S.S. North Carolina Battleship Memorial, which is operated by the State as an educational exhibit. This exhibit is truly for the young people that were not around during World War II, as they try to visual what it must have been like during those days to defend yourself in an ocean full of unfriendly ships. Hopefully, the young people of today will never have to use an instrument of destruction for anything other than defensive purposes.

As we venture into South Carolina, we come to a state that is known for it's outstanding beaches. There are probably very few people in the United States or Canada that has not heard of Myrtle Beach and Hilton Head. With their temperate climate, these beaches enjoy warm breezes from the Gulf Stream and, therefore, are found to be tourist resorts almost year round.

For years, textiles were the main economy for South Carolina. With the influx of foreign textile goods being produced much cheaper, South Carolina has done a phenomenal job in adapting to other industries such as heavy machine manufacturing, rubber goods and electronic products in the more recent past. As textile mills have closed down, there has been a retraining program through the technical education centers scattered throughout the state, that have worked closely with industry. The technical centers retrain these workers for the new industries that are coming into this area of the country. This specialized training has assisted

South Carolina in providing the proper atmosphere and work force to serve the new innovative industries.

In Charleston, South Carolina, we have perhaps one of the best examples of historic preservation of this nations past. Many areas of the city date back to the 1700's and it is possible in walking around the Battery area to visualize how the old sea captains and merchants used to live during times gone by.

In the Greenville area, we find perhaps one of the best water supplies available in the United States. This provides many water impoundments for fishing and recreational purposes, as well as a water supply to support industry. Greenville is perhaps one of the more progressive areas of the country with respect to enticing industry and maintaining a rather low unemployment rate.

As we proceed south into Georgia, we find many similarities with other states of the South. Georgia has fantastic beaches, and beautiful mountains in the western part of the state. Again, we are blessed with the Blue Ridge Mountains that stretch all the way through the South to provide forest product industries with ample wood supplies, and recreational opportunities for the outdoorsman.

With almost 50 per cent of the state forested, it is no wonder that the pulp and paper industry is heavily situated in this southern state.

With the Capitol of the State in Atlanta, we find one of the most modern, progressive Capitol Cities in the South. Atlanta is the corporate headquarters for many national businesses, and provides all of the big city assets, such as art museums, parks, concert facilities, professional sports, and the other positive assets that are so necessary for success. Atlanta at the present time is expanding it's Rapid Transit System to be one of the most modern in the country.

With major seaports in Savannah and Brunswick, the Georgia Ports Authority is rapidly expanding in the field of international trade. As the world proceeds in a positive manner, Georgia has found the ability to adapt and to survive in the changing economy. As we have said about other Southern States, the Southerner with adapt and lead in the development of the future of United States.

For vacation, who hasn't considered going to Florida to enjoy the warm subtropical climate. Along the southern end of the state, we find tropical climates with warm summers and mild winters. With the entire state being somewhat on a coastal plain, we find that the highest point in Florida is in the Northwest and this point rises 345 feet above sea level. As a peninsula jetting 500 miles to the south, Florida has 399 miles of shoreline along the Atlantic Ocean, and 798 miles of shoreline along the Gulf Coast. This would perhaps give you some idea of why commercial and recreational fishing is one of the prime economic factors in this state. Florida has perhaps the widest selection of types of fish both within and off the coast of Florida. This variety of species is wider than any other state in the U.S.

With it's warm tropical climate, the citrus industry is another of the heavy impact areas in the economy of the state. The citrus crop is worth over 500 million dollars a year to this state. Many of our winter vegetables are also grown in South Florida.

A new problem is developing in south Florida which will take considerable study to resolve. Many of the political refugees from the Caribbean have established themselves in the Miami area and this has caused housing and other problems normally associated with a sudden influx of foreigners. Our only hope is that Miami can safely resolve this temporary problem and that these refugees will accept the ways of the United States and try diligently to become active law abiding citizens. The biggest wish is that they will rapidly accept our language, our laws, and our dedication to the Constitution of the United States which obviously was better than the quality of life of the country that they left for our shores.

West Virginia is neither one of the largest states nor one of the most populated states, but it does have the reputation for being the second leading coal producer in the United States. Settled by Welsh, Scotch Irish and Germans, this state certainly had the backbone for hard work. These nationalities were living here when the settlement was founded in 1731. The discovery of coal took place in 1742 when coal was discovered in the Coal River. Since that time, West Virginia has remained a prime supplier of coal for both industrial and residential uses.

As we started this project, I had a young lady from West Virginia call me and asked that unemployment and coal mines not be the only things that we discussed about West Virginia. You cannot discuss West Virginia without discussing coal, but let us look a little further into what other assets West Virginia has developed.

West Virginia is becoming much stronger in the manufacturing field and they have developed tourism to a fine art. There are many parks, flowers, and beautiful homes in the state which should not be overlooked. An asset that they have developed recently is the development of Ski Resort Areas in the mountains. Some of the more popular ski resorts in the south are located in the West Virginia Mountains. With it's beauty, we feel that West Virginia is certainly succeeding in overcoming it's image as nothing but a coal producing state.

Tennessee certainly has a reputation for fine whiskey and country music. Country music is perhaps one of the main contributions that Tennessee has made to the development of America. It is recognized as one of the true American types of music, and country music has been exported worldwide to the delight of those that have listened.

Tennessee shares the Great Smoky Mountains with North Carolina. In addition, Tennessee is blessed with many meandering streams and flat plains suitable for farming. Chief crops raised in Tennessee include soybeans, tobacco and cotton. Originally to assist in agricultural pursuits and irrigation the Tennessee Valley Authority was established to provide power and water control in this state. This state also houses the Oak Ridge National Laboratories for the experimentation and development of Nuclear Energy.

The people of Memphis have harnessed the mighty Mississippi in the development of a project called Mud Island. Sitting on a parcel of land located in the Mississippi River, we find the entire Mississippi River story, from the river history to the Indians and explorers that settled and worked in this area. There are models of the various types of boats that have used the river, both old and new, from the Paddlewheel Steamer to the modern Mississippi Tow Boat. One of the more outstanding developments is a five block long scale model of the entire lower Mississippi River Valley. It is possible to see the river towns layed out to scale adjacent to the river with each of the individual streets in the towns engraved in the metal plates. With the many fairs and festivals that are held on this island, surely you can find some excitement to your liking at this location. If nothing else, you will definitely find the history of the mighty Mississippi to be inspiring.

Certain tourist attractions must be mentioned when we think of Tennessee. Who could forget the dynamic appeal of the following of Elvis Presley. Even though born in Mississippi, he was rapidly accepted by Tennessee. We also think of such patriots as David Crockett, Sam Houston and many of the other "good ole mountain boys" that fought hard to establish the United States as a leader in the world.

When you think of Kentucky, you naturally think of horses. Probably America's most complete Equine complex is found in the Kentucky Horse Park, near Lexington, Kentucky. This horse park is operated by the Commonwealth of Kentucky and is truly a working horse farm. Each building in the complex has a specific function and is used in the actual training and management of the animals housed in this facility. From the Farriers Shop's to the Harness Makers Shop to the Breed Barns, this whole facility is oriented to educating the general public about what is required for the proper care and training of thoroughbreds. Anyone that accepts the horse as one of natures most beautifully designed animals will find something to his liking at this park. There are films, the International Museum of the Horse, and a walking farm tour to visit the various facilities and determine what is required for the proper upkeep of a thoroughbred. Various special events are held at this facility during the course of the year. A trip to this horse park will surely be one of your most enjoyable periods during a visit to Kentucky.

Alabama is definitely deep in the heart of Dixie. With it's colonial mansions and the impressive porticos and porches, we can definitely see the area in which southern gentlemen first arose. Where many of the residents of Alabama still hold on to the beliefs of the old South, many of the younger residents are adapting to the future.

The principle industries within the state include pulp and paper, textiles, and the south's largest producer of iron and steel. With the innovations and cost cutting measures being developed in these industries, Alabama has reluctantly conceded to the future.

One industry that deserves attention is the space and rocket industry located near Huntsville. In this area we find the George C. Marshall Nasa Space Center along with the Alabama Space and Rocket Center in Huntsville. Much of the technology that has allowed the United States to penetrate space and land people on the moon, has been developed in these areas. The Alabama Space and Rocket Center near Huntsville is a tourist facility which allows visitors to examine some of the hardware and technology that has been utilized in our space exploration. With an industry such as this in your back yard, your school systems will prosper and the students will be more inclined to a technologically oriented field.

Alabama has produced such prominent individuals as Hank Aaron, Hugo L. Black, Paul "Bear" Bryant, Nat King Cole, Helen Keller, Jesse Owings and Hank Williams.

With prominent people such as we have just listed, you can see the system in Alabama has produced leaders in many fields for the betterment of the quality of life we presently enjoy.

Mississippi, the Magnolia State, is another southern state steeped in tradition and blessed with the ever present southern mansions. These mansions were usually occupied by large land holders, whose business was to provide the agricultural requirements of the area. Many of the present minorities are direct descendants of slaves that were brought over here by profiteers prior to the Civil War.

One thing that surprised me was to determine that Mississippi is a leading producer of oil and natural gas within the United States. In riding through the state, on occasion I would see an oil or gas well sitting in a field, but I had no idea that they produced such quantities of the products. The majority of this production takes place in the Delta Region near the Gulf Shores.

As we travel around Mississippi, we explore the Florewood River Plantation, which is an authentic recreation of a mid 1850's anti-bellum plantation. This plantation located on the banks of the Yazoo River in the Mississippi Delta Region near Greenwood, appeals to historians, school children, antique buffs, and the romanticists. This plantation is one of Mississippi's most exciting state parks, since it is staffed and operated as a living exhibit. By this, we mean that the Blacksmith Shop, the Potters Shop, and other areas of the plantation have operators that will demonstrate the various crafts and explain how the operation today varies from the operation in the 1800's. Truly, this is one of the interesting spots in Mississippi to visit, since they have constructed 26 buildings as part of the plantation complex.

Originally claimed by the French, and included as part of the Louisiana Purchase in 1803, Louisiana has a definite French background. Along the coastline of Louisiana, we find a group of people called Acadians, which were French settlers that were originally transported from Nova Scotia in Canada. They were forcibly transported to Louisiana and settled the area. As the United States grew, these Acadians became known as Cajuns, and their dialect is still prominent along the Gulf Coast. It has been said that if you once befriend a Cajun, you will have no difficulty in future dealings with any other Acadians.

As we think about Louisiana, events such as the Mardi Gras, Dixie Land Jazz and the French Quarter all pop to mind. Is it any wonder that the late Louis Armstrong was a Louisianian. Where Baton Rouge is the Capitol and the seat of government, New Orleans is the unofficial Queen City that attract the tourist in record numbers.

As with other Gulf Coast States, the topography in Louisiana consist primarily of marshes and Mississippi River flood plain. There are upland hills in the Florida Parishes with an average elevation of 100 feet. The principal industries in Louisiana result in wholesale and retail trade, manufacturing, and transportation. Petroleum also holds a certain impact in the economic analysis of Louisiana.

Located along the Gulf Coast, Louisiana has ports at New Orleans, Baton Rouge, Lake Charles, and the South Louisiana Port Commission at La Place.

While we were visiting Louisiana, we had occasion to visit a Cajun Mardi Gras.

It was during this hometown type Mardi Gras that we had occasion to associate socially with many Acadians that felt strongly regarding their heritage. To me, that is one of the advantages of the United States. People from different national heritage groups can celebrate their own holidays in their own manner.

In New Orleans, we had occasion to celebrate Mardi Gras in a variety of different fashions. We attended a ball for the elite of New Orleans which included all of the engineers, lawyers and other professional type individuals. It was a very formal occasion which included black ties and formal gowns. Even though it was a formal occasion, these people let their hair down to be able to enjoy the festivities of Mardi Gras. In addition, we attended an all girl Mardi Gras Parade. This was an entirely different type of crowd, and a street parade as expected attracted many of the street people that you find in New Orleans. Even though there was a broad mix of personalities, a good time was had by all.

Arkansas offers us long hot summers, mild winters, and abundant rainfall during the year. With these factors in mind, agriculture plays a heavy part in the economic industry of this state. Related industries such as wood and forest products also contribute heavily to their economic well being. Arkansas is first in the mining and production of Bauxite and Bromine. Other mining interests also play a large part in the economic well being of the state.

Where else in the United States, do you find a diamond mine. At the Crater of Diamonds in Murfreesboro, Arkansas, you will find the only diamond mine located in the United States.

Another natural phenomena that occurs in a National Park, occurs at Hot Springs, Arkansas. These baths originally were private developments for supposedly thera-peutic reasons, where people would come and bathe in water that ranged in temperature from 96 degrees to 147 degrees F. Recognizing this to be an phenomena, the National Park Service purchased these establishments in 1921 and began to administer them as a part of the National Park Service. The Park Service entered into a partnership agreement with the bath house concessions in which spring water from a central collection cooling and distribution system was furnished them. The bath houses assumed the responsibility of caring for the bathers.

Another town in Arkansas that I found to be unusual, is the small town of Eureka Springs in Northwest Arkansas. Eureka Springs is built on the side of a mountain with crooked, twisting roads, and little shops built into the side of the hills, up and down the street. Where this is predominently a summer resort area, many people use this area for a getaway weekend. The people are unusually friendly, the scenery is fantastic, and most important, the area is generally relaxing for all.

Virginia

The Victory Monument at Yorktown celebrates the American victory over the British.

Monticello was the home of former President Thomas Jefferson.

The College of William and Mary was the first college established in the United States.

Bruton Parish Church still has regular services today.

60

The Capitol Building in Colonial Williamsburg still flies the British Flag.

The Court House and Powerhorn serve as a museum and living exhibit.

The Governor's Palace is a popular exhibit and features a maze of gardens in the back.

61

North Carolina

The U.S.S. North Carolina Battleship Memorial, a state facility.

Superstructure showing bridge and fire control center.

World War II Kingfisher Aircraft used for scouting and reconnaissance.

Orton House, which was initially constructed around 1735, is located South of Wilmington.

The Scroll Garden is a quiet place for an evening stroll.

The view from the house overlooks the gardens and a wildlife sanctuary.

Luola's Chapel is a quiet place for weddings or meditation.

Many mountain scenes and cabins can be found in Pisgah National Forest.

The Biltmore School of Forestry was started in 1906.

66

Deer are frequently spotted along the roads in the North Carolina Mountains.

A Whitetail Deer catches the evening sun.

Georgia

The restored waterfront area in Savannah.

The Talmadge Bridge spans the Savannah River in Savannah, Georgia.

The waterfront area takes on a different look after dark.

The artistic sculptural carving is the largest of it's kind in the United States.

Dogwoods frame the stone carving on Stone Mountain.

The restored plantation house at Stone Mountain, Georgia.

Various animals can be observed at Stone Mountain.

A train ride takes you around the perimeter of the park.

South Carolina

The steeple of St. Michael's Episcopal Church is seen from many locations in downtown Charleston.

Several beautiful gardens surround the Charleston area.

Bay Street houses are some of the most well preserved and historic in the South.

73

Sunrise on Hilton Head is worth getting up for.

Poinsett Bridge is located in Northern Greenville County.

74

The Triple Crown Races in Aiken attract large crowds in the springtime.

Fishing is a popular pastime as demonstrated here on Clark Hill Lake.

Hampton Plantation, former home of Archibald Rutledge is now a South Carolina State Park.

The Farmer's Society Hall is located in Pendleton.

76

Typical mountain scene in the Whitewater Falls area.

A farmer cuts his hay in the upstate.

77

Florida

Sport fishing is a popular pastime in the Florida Keys.

Fish cleaning time in the Keys.

An Egret watches for his next meal.

Shuttle being readied for launch.

Shuttle take-off sequence.

The oldest house in St. Augustine dates back to the early 1600's.

The original fort at St. Augustine still guards the harbor.

82

Herons at rest.

West Virginia

Railroads serve as a major transportation link in West Virginia.

West Virginia has many mountains, such as these with a snowstorm in the background.

An early spring storm covers this farm with snow.

There are many stately homes in West Virginia.

A portion of the Charleston, West Virginia skyline

This bridge crosses the Monongahela River near Charleston.

This farm represents the quite lifestyle near Morgantown, West Virginia.

Kentucky

My Old Kentucky Home, the plantation that Stephen Foster wrote the song of Kentucky about.

Another view of My Old Kentucky Home showing the Gazebo.

Carriages used in early Kentucky times are on exhibit at the plantation.

The Log Cabin is a reminder of colonial times.

The out buildings continue the architecture of the Horse Park.

The Kentucky Horse Farm is supported by the State of Kentucky.

The tombstone of Man O'War, one of the greatest thoroughbreds to ever run.

90

The International Museum of the Horse features a unique collection of models portraying the horse during various functions.

Even the cupola reflects horse racing.

Visitors have the opportunity to examine the horses closeup.

Tennessee

A monorail delivers you safely to Mud Island.

The Mississippi River is layed out in contour along the Mud Island walkway.

Mud Island at Memphis contains museums, theatres and many fine restaurants.

Memphis is a major port for barge traffic along the Mississippi.

Powerful tugs shift barges around on the Mississippi River.

You do not realize the size of a barge until you see a man hauling a rope on one.

A private vendor makes their living in Nashville.

The Capitol building is impressive when viewed across executive plaza in Nashville.

Nashville is a modern, progressive city.

The Municipal Auditorium host many large events.

Alabama

Most of the rockets from World War II to the present are on display here.

98

The Alabama Space and Rocket Center is located in Huntsville, Alabama.

The Alabama Space and Rocket Center features one of the world's largest collections of space and rocket hardware.

The architecture of the Rocket Center catches the evening sun.

The space and rocket hardware at the Rocket Center can be seen for miles.

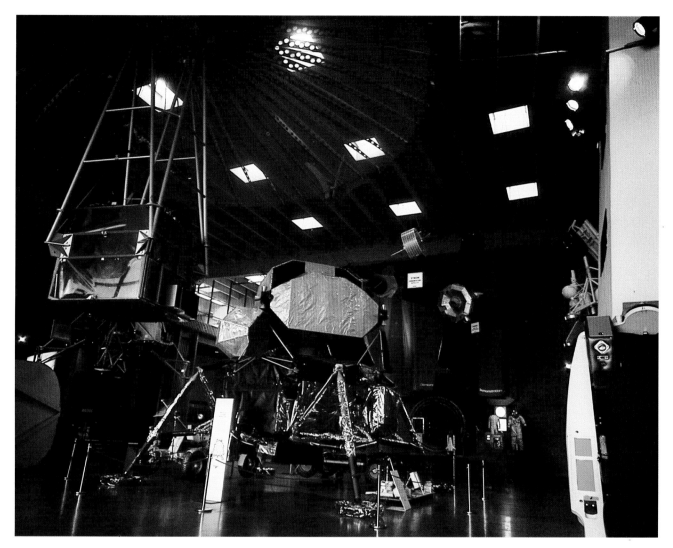

The display area features moon landing devices and other examples of space hardware.

Some of the displays provide the illusion of space travel.

The Church of St. Michael and All Angels, Episcopal, was chartered in 1887.

Arlington Ante-Bellum Home and Gardens, is a fine example of Greek Revival architecture dating from about 1822.

Many mementoes of the Civil War can be seen at Arlington.

Arlington's Gardens are a relaxing place to spend an afternoon.

Mississippi

Antique cannons guard the entrance to the museum.

Old Courthouse Museum in Vicksburg.

McRaven, a civil war home and
gardens on display in Vicksburg.

Illinois Monument to fallen soldiers during the Vicksburg campaign.

Plaque detailing the exploits of the Illinois contingent.

Tilghman Statue of the Vicksburg Battlefield.

Main house, Florewood River Plantation.

Service buildings, Florewood River Plantation near Greenwood, Mississippi.

Buggy used when the plantation was in operation.

The Laundry Room at Florewood was always full of activity.

Typical bedroom at the Florewood Plantation.

Louisiana

Street bands entertained the crowd.

Shangri La Parade in Chalmette.

It's Mardi Gras time in New Orleans.

*Two young men enjoying themselves
at the Cajun Mardi Gras.*

"Take my picture, make me famous"

*Everyone participates in the Cajun
Mardi Gras.*

Comic character created by Blaine Kern at the Bacchus Ball.

Another Blaine Kern creation at the ball.

Arkansas

Even the springs were artistic in the 1920's.

The countryside near Eureka.

The landscaping around the baths was most relaxing.

The Hot Springs Rehabilitation Center has the best view in town.

116

The Maurice Baths is an example of the former resort establishments, now part of the National Park in Hot Springs.

The Basin Park Hotel in Eureka is now a Museum.

117

Buckstaff Baths is another example of the baths found in Hot Springs.

The Great Lakes Area

Like a wagon hub with spokes generating outward in all directions, the Great Lakes States are the hub of industrial activity in the United States. With it's link to the sea by way of the St. Lawrence Seaway, the Great Lakes area has developed into a series of large port facilities in which ore, grain, and industrial products are shipped all over the world. Where this shipping activity is centered in the major port facilities, the people have also radiated out and a great deal of farming also takes place in the outer reaches of this area. The area has been settled predominately by Germans, Irish, and Welch. We even ran into a Finnish Community in central Minnesota. It is truly unique when we realize how many ethnic and cultural backgrounds make up the population of the United States.

While exploring Minnesota, we came upon the town of Two Rivers along the shore. They were celebrating the Bicentennial of their town, so therefore we found the people in an extremely amiable mood. Two Rivers was the shipping point for many tons of ore that left through their harbor facilities. Being directly on Lake Superior, they had access to worldwide ports through the lakes chain. As part of their celebration, they had the tug "Edna G" brightly painted and on display for the local towns people to visit. The "Edna G" has been retired from service and now serves only as a local monument. Adjacent to the harbor, we found the Railroad Museum with one of the largest steam locomotives ever to serve in the United States on display along with one of the old antique locomotives. In the immediate area, we found ore cars and even sleighs that we used to bring workers to the mines during periods of heavy snow.

The port of Duluth is one of the busiest ports on the Great Lakes. Being a heavy industrialized city, it would be primarily an attraction to those who appreciate cities.

Wisconsin is the next state that we come to in our travels in the Great Lakes Region. Wisconsin was originally settled by French Missionaries, followed closely behind by fur traders. The British then controlled Wisconsin for a period of time until the United States took the land during the war of 1812. It became a part of the United States in 1848. In earlier days, iron mines and farming provided a major portion of the states economy. At the present time, manufacturing and transportation, along with agriculture, provide the principal industries that create income for Wisconsin at this time.

In our travels around the state, we found many attractive locations. One of the prettiest spots that we found in all of Wisconsin was located near Upper and Lower Devils Lakes at a campground. With a clean lake covered with canoes

119

and fishing boats, we had some of our most restful moments on the trip here. Added to this, we met some very interesting people that allowed us to photograph the sunset from their campsite. As we have stated before, one of the big fringes to our travels throughout the United States has been the opportunity to meet the interesting people that we have encountered and to get their views on what they think about these United States.

Another spot in Wisconsin that attracts quite a bit of attention are the Wisconsin Dells, where a fast moving river has etched sandstone into elaborate natural statues. The town of Wisconsin Dells is very much tourist oriented, but I think this is predominate in every state that we visited. If there was a natural wonder to attract the people, then the commercial tourist attractions followed close behind. This is not to criticize the tourist industry, but only to note that within the United States this is a natural phenomena. You will be able to find accommodations and other points of interest.

In Michigan, you are in a state that has the longest shoreline of any inland state within the United States. Michigan can boast of 2,232 miles of shoreline and is touched by four of the five Great Lakes. Lake Ontario is the only lake that does not join Michigan at some point. In addition to great lakes shipping, Michigan is famous for it's production of automobiles and paper. From the Gerald R. Ford Museum in Grand Rapids to Holland, Michigan, we are able to visualize the Dutch influence by the prolific growing of flowers in this area. We also encounter lighthouses on inland seas to warn lake travelers. At the north end of the state, we find the Great Mackinac Straits Bridge which goes to the upper peninsula of Michigan. Michigan is indeed blessed with many beautiful spots.

We met a couple at the Grand Canyon in Arizona and informed them of our tentative route through Michigan. After some conversation, they informed us that we were going to several unattractive areas. They marked up a map for us and we have attempted to follow this map to the spots that they felt we would find some of the most beautiful scenes in Michigan. Their main concern was that they did not want to show Michigan and the unemployment situation that has been prolific in recent years. For their assistance, we wish to thank them because they certainly lead us to some fantastic spots in Michigan.

We also ran into a young woman in Petoskey, Michigan who had some strong feelings on how young people should be treated and respected for their views on the future of America.

In Ohio, we come to the state that is ranked sixth by population with a 1980 census figure of 10,797,419 people. These people are involved in manufacturing, mining and agriculture and are deeply rooted in their dedication to the state.

Where we thought that Vermont and New Hampshire had the concession on covered bridges, we were sadly mistaken. At a friends suggestion, we visited Ashtabula County in Ohio and found that there were approximately 22 covered bridges in this area. They range from short ones to very long ones and just about every type of construction known for covered bridges. If you take the time to look them up, it is truly a sight to reflect on the past.

In Columbus, we found a very impressive State Capitol Building. In our venture around the State Capitol, we found statues and mementos from the past history of Ohio that literally told the tale of it's struggle for independence. Columbus also has a very attractive Museum of Art that is well worth the time if you take it.

In Indiana, we came across Thomas Lincoln's Farm near Dale, Indiana. This recreated settlement showed us how Lincoln must have lived in his growing years, splitting rails and farming for survival. With the work that had to be accomplished with the crude tools that were available it is no wonder that Abraham Lincoln grew up to be man enough to shoulder the job of Presidency. Also in this area, you will find Nancy Hanks Lincoln's grave on the premises.

In Illinois, we find Chicago, the queen city of activity on the great lakes. As the center of activity, it also is the hub of all transportation and manufacturing represented by the great lakes area.

We also find the continuing trail of Abraham Lincoln. In Springfield, in a preserved section of the old town, we find the only house that Abraham Lincoln ever owned. Authentic detail has been preserved in this house all the way down to the curtains on the windows. As you stroll down the gravel streets of the preserved section, you can literally transform yourself back into Lincoln's time to mentally visualize how things must have been during his period of rise to prominence.

As we rode around the southern part of Illinois, we were able to observe the agricultural activity that is still prominent in this area. Having had the opportunity to view agriculture in it's various stages throughout the seasons this year, we know for a fact that farmers certainly earn the money that they make.

We also found in this state, a small college in Eureka. It would not be noteworthy to mention the fact that Eureka, Illinois has a small college except that this is the college that provided the advanced educational opportunities that were afforded to President Ronald Reagan in his developmental years. Having talked with the people and visited in the town, it is possible to understand where he developed many of his priorities that he has accepted to live his life by.

In general, we would have to sum up the great lakes area as being almost the backbone of industry in the United States. In addition, we would also recognize that a great deal of agriculture is accomplished in this area. With the people that we encountered, I feel that these people represent a major part of the population that makes up the backbone of the United States. They certainly adhere to the standards which we so proudly display for the rest of the world.

Minnesota

*During their Bicentennial, Two Rivers, Minnesota had a Coast Guard Cutter
and the "Edna G" for boarding.*

*On touring the local museum, we find the "Edna G" in miniature with many other
historical items.*

A threatening storm on the horizon north of Cloquet will give farmers much needed rain.

A peaceful farm is symbolic of Minnesota's farming influence.

123

Duluth is one of the busier port facilities on Lake Superior.

One of the many streams and waterfalls that provides beauty and entertainment for all in Minnesota.

124

Wisconsin

The fishing is apparently outstanding on Rice Lake.

The Public Library in Wisconsin Dells is extremely popular with the local people.

Wisconsin Dells offers something for all the tourist that come to visit.

The building facades spell out the variety of businesses in Wisconsin Dells.

126

Michigan

The restored light keepers quarters in Eagle Harbor was constructed in 1851.

The American Flag flies proudly at Eagle Harbor Lighthouse.

127

The skyline of Grand Rapids reflects from the windows of the President Gerald R. Ford Museum.

The Dutch influence is very prominent in Holland, as we see in this view of City Hall.

128

Two anchors at the Maritime Park frame the Mackinaw Bridge in northern Michigan.

This lumberjack in Cadillac is symbolic of the pride of the northern Michigan woodsman.

Ohio

This is typical of the many covered bridges found in Ashtubula County, Ohio.

Snow only enhances the beauty of these covered bridges.

130

The Ohio State Capitol shrouded in fog is still the seat of government.

The Columbus Museum of Art is well worth the effort.

Indiana

Near Dale, Indiana, Abraham Lincoln spent his boyhood in a farm similar to this.

The original foundation for the Lincoln Farmhouse is located on this property.

The animal shed was used to feed and shelter the horses and livestock that they owned.

The Lincoln cabin was similar to that on this living farm.

Nancy Hanks Lincoln is buried on the National Park Service grounds nearby.

Illinois

The Lincoln House in Springfield is the only house that President Abraham Lincoln ever owned.

In the Lincoln House, we find that authentic detail even includes the curtains.

In southern Illinois, farming is a major input to the economy.

Farmers have extremely rich soil in which to grow their crops.

135

Eureka College can claim President Ronald Reagan as one of it's alumni.

The wishing well holds fond memories for many of Eureka College's students.

136

The Plains States

Agriculture is the key word in all of the Plains States. You cannot think about this area without thinking about crops, yields, livestock, and farm machinery. One only has to ride through these states in the summer and see all of the rich crops in all of their splendor to understand that this area feeds a good majority of the population of the United States. Many plains farmers had pride in their voice as they told me about the life on the plains and number of people that they fed.

Since wheat farming plays a big part in the crops in the northern plains states, we selected one farm in North Dakota to try and show in depth the various activities that take place during a wheat farming operation. The farm that we selected was near Jamestown, North Dakota. It was through a mutual friend that I was granted permission to visit this area and take pictures of eight identical combines working in the same field. As I strolled around the field taking pictures of the various machines in operation, I felt extremely insignificant in the whole makeup of the things that were taking place. Each worker or operator knew exactly what was expected of him, knew how to accomplish this feat, and went about their chores with no instructions from the leader. It appeared to me to be tremendous tribute to the farmer that was able to farm this many acres with such a relative small crew as efficiently as they operated. As we rode through other plains states with wheat farming operations underway, we did not attempt to duplicate what we found in North Dakota, but felt that we could explain that the same type of operation was taking place in South Dakota, Nebraska, Oklahoma, Iowa, and several of the other states in this area. We hope you enjoy our close up viewpoint of wheat farming.

In Nebraska and Iowa, we found that corn soon took the place of wheat farming in these areas. We were able to record areas in Kansas that a drought has affected the crop production.

While doing research for this book, we discovered that South Dakota has a population density of only 8.9 people per square mile. This is not very significant until you think about New York City with it's population density of 23,494 people per square mile. The population density of the entire United States, based on the 1980 census, converts to 64 people per square mile. This tells me that less people are producing more because they can see their accomplishments growing in the field. With this in mind, shouldn't we provide fair price support systems for our farmers?

If we look in the area of Amana, Iowa, we see a tremendous Amish colony that has developed a cooperative farming effort and still maintains their ability to practice their religion as they see fit. It is said by some that the soil in Iowa is probably some of the richest in America. The states high crop yield supports the nations largest livestock industry.

In Oklahoma, all of the citizens are proud of the fact that they have an oil field under the State Capitol. Oklahoma has many rich oil fields that are seen from time to time throughout the countryside. In southern Oklahoma, there were many cotton fields that were in full bloom. We observed that they are now using mechanical pickers to harvest their crop.

In Nebraska, as in other plains states, they grow a tremendous amount of corn and other vegetables. Agriculture is the major industry in this state and everyone of it's residents are oriented or directly affected by what happens to the agricultural market. Typical of the landmarks that you find in Nebraska which date back to early exploratory days you find Chimney Rock. Located near the North Platt River Valley, Chimney Rock was one of the most celebrated of all natural formations along the overland routes to California, Oregon and Utah. As an early landmark, the solitary spire marked the end of plains travel and the beginning of the rugged mountain portion of their journey. Thousands of travelers carved their names in the soft base of the spire only to have these names disappear through the forces of nature. The eroded landmark is smaller than that which greeted the early visitors, but it's presence for the generations of the near future is secure.

As we entered Kansas, we arrived at Fort Scott, which was originally built around 1846. This fort was built from native materials of walnut, ash and oak that grew thickly along the bottom lands of Marmaton. The fort at that time consisted of barracks, houses for the officers, stables for the horses, a hospital, a magazine and various store houses. At the present time, Fort Scott is maintained by the National Park Service as a living exhibit and during the season you have actors that portray occupants of the fort. As we walk around the fort we can visualize how the inhabitants must have lived and we see replicas of the tools that they utilized during their time. A stop at Fort Scott is definitely worth the time.

Next, we come to the "Cathedral of the Plains" in Victoria, Kansas. This structure was erected between 1908 and 1911 by German and German-Russian Catholics. It is one of the largest buildings on the great plains and it's twin towers soar 141 feet above it foundations. This structure has been approved and is on the registry of National Historic Places in the United States.

As we move on through Kansas to Abilene, we find the Eisenhower Center and "Place of Meditation." The original Eisenhower home has been preserved and maintained and with the addition of a museum, library, and place of meditation, the stop is well worth the time. It is particularly impressive to me to see where presidents have had their roots and what kind of area was a basis for the formation of feelings about people and world affairs.

One of the more pleasant surprises that occurred to us in our travels around the country occurred in Fulton, Missouri when we discovered the Winston Churchill Memorial and Library at Westminister College. This memorial originally started life in London, England and was designed by Sir Christopher Wren, whose skill and artistry were unrivaled. A 12th Century staircase utilized in the original structure is intact to this day. In 1940, this historic sanctuary was struck by a German incendiary bomb. After the fires had been extinguished, all that remained of Wren's masterpiece were the outside walls, a bell tower and twelve stone columns. The church was never rebuilt in London. It was after World War II that a memorial committee headed by President John F. Kennedy proposed to bring it to the United States as an eternal reminder of the inter-dependence of the English-Speaking people. The church was eventually rebuilt at a cost of $1,300,000, which was raised in the United States. The church was re-dedicated on the Campus of Westminister College in 1946. This is truly worth the time and I would recommend it to everyone who has any allegiance to this country.

Another spot that gave us some insight into how the United States has risen with pride is the George Washington Carver Monument in this state. This monument is to a man who was born a slave and rose to national prominence by age 55. Predominantly known as an Educator, Botanist, Agronomist, he was also known to his friends as an artist. He was to many young blacks an encouraging model who set standards to which they could aspire. This monument is worthwhile exposure of his efforts to improve both his race and the understanding between races and to his tremendous talent in the field of research.

As we move on to Texas, we are moving into the state that is the third most populated in the United States. We also are moving into the state that is the second largest in area with 267,338 square miles of territory. Even at this, the population density is only 53.2 people per square mile.

We are talking about a state with as many diverse interest and assets as you might find in many of the remaining states. You could do a book on the entire state of Texas and you would end up leaving some part of it out. To properly cover Texas we have tried to include scenes that are indicative of the sights, sounds and smells that you would find within the state. As you look through the pictures, try to imagine what we were thinking when we saw all of these magnificent things of beauty.

North Dakota

These pictures are dedicated to all of the wheat farmers throughout the plains area. This particular set of photographs was taken near Jamestown, North Dakota during a combine operation.

Wind Canyon in Theodore Roosevelt National Park is an area subjected to high winds.

The winds, and not man, have caused the decorative erosion that has taken place in Wind Canyon.

142

South Dakota

Washington, Jefferson, Roosevelt and Lincoln are the Presidents that are forever carved in the face of Mt. Rushmore.

A colorful park greets you at Mt. Rushmore.

A wheat field awaits the combines approach.

Combines at rest awaiting their next challenge.

144

Sunflowers are an attractive cash crop for Plains farmers.

A sunflower poses for the photographer.

145

Iowa

Moonrise over a sleeping corn field.

Far Left. *Corn is one of the primary crops in the State of Iowa.*

Left. *An ear of corn is unknown in many European countries.*

146

Typical grain bins near Arcadia, Iowa.

147

Wind vain and cupola in Amana, Iowa.

Silos near Arcadia stand tall against a blue sky.

Sprinklers are frequently used to improve crop harvest.

Oklahoma

An oil drilling crew works late in the night to bring in a gusher.

Mechanical cotton picking is prominent in the southern part of Oklahoma near Altus.

With this rig, many cotton pickers lost their jobs.

The Oklahoma State Capitol is located over an active oil field in Oklahoma City.

The Oklahoma Museum of Natural History is located near the State Capitol.

152

An oil well pumps oil on the Capitol grounds.

The bronc buster is located on the grounds of the Capitol.

153

Nebraska

The spire at Chimney Rock is visible for miles.

Corn is a popular crop near Scottsbluff, Nebraska.

This award-winning bridge is found along Route 26 in Nebraska.

This wheat is heavy and ready for the combine.

Golden fields such as this are prominent in late summer.

Kansas

The Cathedral of the Plains in Victoria is one of the tallest structures in this area.

This local statue in Victoria is dedicated to early inhabitants of this area.

157

Fort Scott is a recreation of the original fort located in this area.

Housewares and the actual utensils used by occupants are intact.

Farm implements used during the period of Fort Scott are on display.

The type of tankards used in the tavern can be found at this living fort.

The Place of Meditation is the final resting place of President Eisenhower and his wife Mamie.

The Eisenhower home place in Abilene is part of the Dwight D. Eisenhower Library Complex.

160

Missouri

This statue of George Washington Carver is located near Joplin in the area that he grew up in.

As he matured, George Washington Carver spent his adult teaching years at Tuskegee Institute.

161

The Churchill Memorial in Fulton was a Christopher Wren Church moved from London.

The Ten Commandments behind the pulpit are a constant reminder to those that attend church here.

162

The detail within the Churchill Memorial Complex in Fulton is as close as possible to the original Christopher Wren design.

Near the pulpit, we find the American Flag which stands for freedom of religion.

The spiral staircase found in the Churchill Memorial dates back several centuries.

Texas

This scene is typical in a good many places in Texas.

Golden fields are found in northern Texas where wheat is grown.

Windmills are popular for pumping water in remote areas of the range in Texas.

165

Rolls of hay dot the Texas countryside.

A pair of oil pumping rigs are decorated to amuse the traveler.

The Mountain States

As civilization pushed Westward, the mountains proved to be the most formidable barrier that the early settlers encountered. As we travel these areas on paved roads, we should reflect back to what it must have been like for Lewis and Clark during their times with no roads, no bridges or other engineering achievements to make their way easier. Wild animals, primitive firearms, and hostile Indians did little to improve their chances of survival. Perhaps if we had to cross the country under similar circumstances, our generation might have a deeper appreciation of nature, and it's manner of throwing the elements against the humans that dare to invade it.

In Northern Idaho's panhandle section, we find a beautiful town at Coeur d'Alene. Even though our visits were in March and July, we found the town to be warm, friendly and the people to be extremely hospitable. In an area as remote as this is, the people learn to depend on one another for strength and this gives them the character that they exhibit to visitors. Lake Coeur d'Alene and Lake Pend Oreille along with Farragut State Park serve to attract visitors to this area during the summer months for the recreational opportunities.

As we move further south in the state, we come into the farming areas and into the industrial areas. We hit there during a period of snow, and were greeted with smooth unbroken lines, storm clouds, and one of the most peaceful feelings that you can experience on a trip. Near Idaho Falls, we had an occasion to talk with some of the local people and found that they had basically the same priorities that people in the deep south have. Freedom to express themselves, freedom to live their lives the way that they desired to live them, and pride in the United States were the main thoughts that were expressed to us.

We had a barber in Kent, Washington tell us that when we got to Montana that we should not miss Flathead Lake. Having followed hunches like this from other people, we made our way to Polson, which is in the Northwest corner of Montana. Flathead Lake and the river that forms the lake runs through Flathead Valley. Flathead Valley is a scenic agriculture, outdoor, and recreation area.

Proceeding south from Polson, we came to the National Bison Range, which is in Moiese, Montana. This range was established as a part of a permanent home for the preservation of wildlife whose numbers were in serious problems with the changes that were made in the habitat, or the areas occupied by the wildlife. As land use is revised from time to time, this changes the feeding patterns and some animals who prefer a particular type of food are left out when the changes take place. Bison, or the American Buffalo, were hunted to near extinction near

167

the turn of the century. Not only were they killed for food, but many of them were destroyed just for the sake of killing wildlife. It was a tremendous waste of this magnificent animal.

While on the National Bison Range, we had occasion to observe Elk with the horns in velvet. These Elk were found peacefully grazing along one of the access roads through the range. In addition, we spotted many Antelope which were beautifully marked. We also had the opportunity of watching the Buffalo herd come roaring across one of the hills to water. Unless you have seen over 400 Buffalo in a single herd thundering through the dust across a field, that is a sight that you can only imagine. On the edge of the National Bison Range, we had occasion to see a Whitetail Deer with twin fawns. The doe was carefully picking it's way up a creek with the fawns faithfully following behind. We hope that when you look at the pictures of the National Bison Range that you will be able to imagine the excitement that we felt when we saw these magnificent animals closeup.

As we left the Bison Range, we came to the town of St. Ignatius. From the signs on the highway, we determined that this was the location of the St. Ignatius Mission, which was established in 1854. This mission was established to quiet the repeated request of Indians, who journeyed from the Rocky Mountains to St. Louis, for someone to bring religion to this area. This beautiful church that remains is one sign of the faith and devotion of the Indian people. They, with their missionaries, built this church in 1891 with local materials. From the exterior, St. Ignatius Mission does not give the impression of being any different from any one of a number of frontier churches that had been established. Once you step inside, you see a collection of murals that were designed and painted by Brother Joseph Carignano, the mission cook. The beautiful paintings are all over 70 years old. This church remains to the present day, the religious center of the Flathead Indian people.

After meandering through the northern part of Colorado, we came to Mesa Verde National Park. This area is famous for the group of Indians who lived in the four corners country that picked Mesa Verde for their home. It is not known why they chose this particular lifestyle, but it has been determined that they lived and prospered on the Verde and in it's canyons. These dwelling have been deserted since the end of the thirteenth century. The people lived in these caves, that had been hollowed out by wind and erosion, and built their dwelling to utilize the protection of the overhang. It was common in those times to plant their crops on top of the Mesa and to build their homes under the Mesa. Perhaps this is one of life's curiousities that we may never know the complete answer too, but it certainly tells us a little bit about how some of our ancestors reasoned things out.

You cannot discuss the State of Utah without giving some mention regarding the Mormon influence or the Latter Day Saints Churches presence in this state. Like any other religion within the United States, individual church demonations are free to worship as they wish and the Latter Day Saints church is no different from Mennonite, Christian, or and of the other religions that might be present within this country. Where we saw many Latter Day Saints Churches within Utah and around the rest of the country, we selected the church in Logan, Utah to be symbolic of this religion in this state. It is a very attractive structure sitting on a hill overlooking the town, and has a place of distinction in the hearts of everyone within this area.

While in Park City, Utah, we had an occasion to go up in a hot air balloon for a birds eye view of some of the ski areas. If you have never been, a hot air balloon ride is something that you should not pass up should you get the opportunity. We noticed in the town of Park City that where the original mining village has been upgraded to a ski resort, they have attempted to hold on to some of the original architectural features of the mining community. In this age in which so many historic relics and buildings have been demolished in favor of glass and steel structures, we would applaud Park City for their foresight in the marriage of old and new into the renovation of their town.

In the western park of Utah, we were looking forward to seeing the famous Bonneville Salt Flats where all of the world speed records, for several years, had been set. Much to our amazement, the Bonneville Salt Flats were another inland sea of many acres of water. It was explained to us that the Bonneville Salt Flats had been subjected to run off from snow melt for several years and now had a covering of water that had no place to go. They estimate that the water that is currently covering the Bonneville Salt Flats will take up to ten years to evaporate before the salt flats are again available for racing.

New Mexico offers us three major cultures; Spanish, Indian and Angelo American. We also find within this state the nations largest Indian Reservation. The reservation is a Navajo Reservation and it is comprised of several million acres.

In this area of the country, people tend to be less suspicious and more open to strangers since they have few of the big city life type of pressures on them. We also find that the relaxing mood of the mountains and valleys tend to cause the human mind to relax and accept things as they are. In the higher altitudes, you do not find people running around because it would take them too long to catch their breath. In general, this area and it's scenery tends to cause a very relaxed way of life.

One only has to visit Sante Fe, New Mexico to be able to get a glimpse of this relaxed lifestyle. From the peppers drying in the sun to the vendors sitting in the shade selling their handmade trinkets, you are able to see all around you a layed back form of life. It possesses it's own beauty in that there is a difference in the lifestyle that they have out here, the houses built from adobe to withstand the elements, and in general the relaxed way of life to keep them from over exerting themselves in the heat.

Once outside of Sante Fe, we begin to see the mountains and rolling hills that tell you that you are in a remotely populated area, where the environment can be harsh and unforgiving until you learn to adapt. Some of the smaller towns will never grow much larger unless they discovered a water supply that will provide them with one of the basic necessities for life.

In Northern Nevada, we find the same type of atmosphere that we find in other mountain states, in that we have impressive mountains and a pretty relaxed life-style. In the area around Lake Tahoe, the accumulation of winter snow has brought the development of ski resorts, but they do not disrupt the lifestyle. I think the skiers are able to appreciate the value of the peaceful attitude in the mountains and therefore the skiing is relaxing. In Southern Nevada, we have Las Vegas. Las Vegas, a resort city, has an entirely different personality from other areas in Nevada. With it's bright lights, and colorful gambling casinos, Las Vegas is a city predominently aimed at tourist and their pleasures. This is not to say that the local people living in Las Vegas year round are all hustlers, gamblers and hookers. These people just have different professions and a different lifestyle from some of their more contemporary neighbors. Most of the local people that I met that lived north of the gambling casinos, and said that they seldom, if ever, go into the casinos to partake of the festive atmosphere.

The Grand Tetons and Yellowstone are two of the most impressive sights that we encountered in Wyoming. The Grand Tetons as they rise from the valley floor to their majestic heights proudly proclaim their dominence within the area. One only has to imagine this area in the winter time with several feet of snow to understand the harsh life that earlier settlers experienced in this area. Only the very strongest of these people were able to survive.

As you move further north into Yellowstone National Park, you begin to see to force of the rivers and the way they have gouged canyons within the park. This combined with the beautiful mountain ranges gives you a strong feeling of the force of nature. Within the expanse of Yellowstone, if you are observant you can spot many forms of wildlife. Among those we spotted were Moose, Elk, Buffalo, Deer and other assorted small animals. This area has been a favorite of visitors for many years and you find them rafting the rivers and fishing the streams. You only have to be in the area for a few hours to realize that this is a part of America that is special. It is one of the reasons that Americans take pride in the country as well as the people. You cannot visit this area without feeling a sense of pride or pleasure in knowledge that we in the United States have a treasure such as this in our own backyard.

As we enter Arizona, we immediately know that there is something special about this state. From the Saguaro National Forest to Tuscon to the Painted Desert to the Petrified Forest and up to the Grand Canyon, we see geologic treasures that cannot be duplicated elsewhere. Starting with Saguaro National Monument, it is in this area that we have protected the magnificent stand of Saguaro Cactus that can range in height to between 30 and 40 feet. While visiting this area, we were able to observe a birds nest that had been hollowed out of the soft pulp in the center of the cactus, and observe biddies within the nest. If you get there early in the morning, you can see the cactus blooming in the spring of the year. We were also impressed by the Arizona-Sonora Desert Museum, which is almost adjacent to the Saguaro National Monument. This Museum is perhaps one of the most complete and thoroughly informative living museums that I have ever had occasion to visit. Just about every form of bug, insect, animal, and plant that you experience in the local desert is included here. At the Desert Museum, outside you will see all of the living animals that you will normally find in the Sonoran Desert region. Once you enter the museum, you will examples of the bugs, spiders, and other insects and creatures that inhabit this desert region. You will also find an example of just about every kind of gemstone that is found in this region. Again, as we have stated, it is one of the most informative museums that we have ever encountered.

Riding through the Painted Desert and Petrified Forest, you see examples of geologic formations that are predominent primarily in this area. It is extremely hard to realize that a colorful rock such as these could have been part of a tree many centuries ago.

As we travel north we see beautiful rock outcrops that are further evidence of the harshness of the environment in this area.

To be able to visit the Grand Canyon is an adventure unto itself. As you pick up information regarding the canyon, you will learn that the canyon can be as much seven miles wide at some points. As you look at the canyon and spot the Colorado River, looking at the depth of the canyon you can imagine the force that this river exerts on the walls of the canyon. Whether you are there in the winter or the summer, a beautiful sight awaits you. We truly hope that you will enjoy the sights that we found during our visit.

While at the Grand Canyon, we met the wife of a local cowboy. She explained to us the harshness of life on a ranch in this area. She explained that water was almost inaccessible due to the extreme depth that you would have to drill to reach it. She explained that a tanker truck delivered water to them and it was pumped into a storage tank. This water was then used for the household use and watering the livestock. The tanker brought in roughly 10,000 gallons once a week, which meant that they had to ration the water for their use. It was really interesting to hear someone talk about the scarcity of water and how they have to exist from week to week on what they have. We hope that everyone in this country would appreciate the value of water and what it can do for them.

Idaho

On Lake Coeur D'Alene, boating is a very serious activity.

In Coeur d'Alene, Idaho, they even decorate the town clock with the American Flag, which flies so proudly.

On an otherwise cold day, this red barn along Route 20 seem to add some warmth.

Driving North on Highway 20, the blowing snow gave a strange sensation to the traveler.

Many Idaho towns are nestled at the base of the mountains.

The sun peeking through the snow clouds gives a different view of the mountains.

174

Montana

St. Ignatius Mission was founded in
1854 to serve the Salish and Kootenai
Indian Tribes.

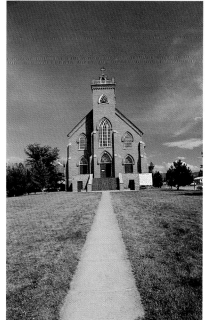

The interior of the Church was painted at night by a cook as his contribution
to this mission.

A cow and a bull Elk graze peacefully in the National Bison Range.

Whitetail Doe and two Fawns are caught sneaking up a stream bed.

Right. *Antelope can be seen throughout the National Bison Range.*

Below. *As the herd rushes across the range, a cloud of dust is kicked up.*

A typical Montana scene with all of the natural ingredients.

Flat Falls along the Kootenai River.

Colorado

Cliff Dwellings at Mesa Verde National Park.

Cliff Dwellings were last inhabited during the Thirteenth Century.

Snow capped mountain scenery near Berthoud Pass.

Interstate Highway System near Denver.

Utah

As we look at the hand of the balloonist operating the controls, we view the inside of the largest balloon of it's type.

When several balloons get together, it's fun for all involved.

182

From a balloon the ski trails of Park City stand out clearly.

Park City, originally a mining town, has mixed old and new architecture.

183

They estimate that it will be ten years before the moisture evaporates from Bonneville Salt Flats.

Flooded pasture east of Logan is an impressive sight to the visitor, not to the farmer.

184

The Latter Day Saints Church in Logan, Utah is majestic looking from the hilltop.

New Mexico

In front of the Palace of the Governors in Sante Fe, the Indians sell their handmade crafts.

The town square in Sante Fe is a popular meeting place.

The Museum of Fine Arts and Museum of New Mexico are located on the town square in Sante Fe.

Outside of the Museum of Fine Arts we find clowns at work.

187

Open courtyards are decorated with the cities past.

Red peppers hang to dry before being used.

The mountains near Raton frequently are covered with snow.

Nevada

From a lofty perch you can see all of Las Vegas.

Las Vegas retains the look of the olden times in some of it's casinos.

You will find new and old construction on the same street.

The Hotels and Casinos glow with light after dark.

Snow capped mountains near Lake Tahoe present a wintry scene.

Wyoming

Yellowstones spectacular Lower Falls are impressive even on a rainy day.

J. Pierce Cunningham Cabin is located at the base of the Grand Tetons.

A Bull Moose can frequently weigh in
excess of 1200 pounds.

Two fly fishermen enjoy the pleasure of Yellowstone's streams.

Floating the Snake River in rafts is fun for the whole family.

A Chipmunk puts on a show.

Arizona

The Grand Canyon at sunset is as pretty as any place you might want to visit.

196

The Painted Desert has undergone many changes over the years.

The Petrified Forest gives us examples of our prehistoric past.

198

The Grand Canyon with a coat of snow presents a different face.

Every observation point at the Grand Canyon gives you a different view.

Outside of the National Park the Canyon is still visible, only in much smaller dimensions.

The Baby Rocks create an unusual rock outcrop.

Many types of desert animals can be seen at the Arizona-Sonora Desert Museum.

The Pacific States

As we look at the Pacific States, the first thing that we notice is that three of the states are part of the contiguous United States and two states are entirely separated from the rest of the nation. We will look at Alaska and Hawaii last since each of them have special geologic or personality aspects that deserve separate mention.

As we look at California, we are looking at the state that is ranked first in population with a 1980 census population of 23,668,562 people. Since California is also the third largest state, they end up with a population density of 149.1 people per square mile. The population is pretty much centered in the southern part of the state where the climate is a little more acceptable to a larger majority of the people. In addition, the Los Angeles area is pretty well inundated with factories and industries that require the people for operation of their facilities.

In looking at California more closely, we find that California has 1,264 miles of some of the prettiest coastline that you have ever seen. This coastline ranges anywhere from rock outcrops where the mountains touch the sea to sandy beaches in areas where the slope is a little more gentle. As you work your way east, you hit an extreme with the lowest spot in the United States in Death Valley. In the northern part of California we have wooded areas and some of the most beautiful scenery and farms that you can imagine.

Perhaps one of the jewels in California lies in Yosemite National Park. In this area made famous by Ansel Adams, in his sensitive photographs of renown places such as Half Dome, Rainbow Falls and El Capitan, and other equally prominent features, we find nature at its finest. The natural beauty of the mountains and valleys in Yosemite are beyond description until you have had the opportunity to experience them for yourself. We only hope that our photographs will give you some idea of what you can anticipate with respect to this work of nature.

Oregon is a state that is based entirely on nature, in that it's major industry is forestry and forest products. In addition, we see an abundant usage of harnessing the power of the Columbia River for the generation of electricity. As you watch the Columbia River travel down the Columbia Gorge, again this is an example of the force of the river carving at the rock outcrops and developing another excellent example of the magically works of nature. As you cross Oregon's Mountains to get to the eastern part of the state, you find yourself in an area void of substantial vegetation and bordering on a desert type environment. It is in these areas that you see cattle being raised that have adapted themselves to the tough wire grass and other meager vegetation available in this area. I think that it would be close to estimate that 75 per cent of the population lives in 25 per cent of the lush green western coastline.

Washington State is the only state in the nation that offer you the Cascades, Whidbey Island, and the impressive skyline of Seattle, one of the busiest ports on the west coast.

North of Seattle you find Whidbey Island. Ferry service from Everett is available to the south end of the island and there is a bridge at Deception Pass that connects the Island to Anacortes, Washington. While on Whidbey Island, visit Fort Casey State Park, which is midway of the island. This fort was used until World War II in defense of the attack that was anticipated, but never occurred. One of the highlights of a visit to the fort will be the display of 2–10″ "Disappearing Guns." They are thought to be the only ones of this size still in existence.

Another interesting spot in Washington is Rocky Reach Dam, which is just north of Wenatchee. With the beautiful picnic areas and the grounds adjoining the dam facility, you can plan on spending several hours at this spot. One of the more impressive floral displays is available for viewing at this dam. Be sure not to miss the American Flag done in flowers at this point. For the sportsman that might be in the crowd, there are fish viewing windows within the dam to allow you to watch salmon swimming upstream to return to their breeding grounds.

First in area, last in population, this is Alaska. Alaska is truly one of the last frontiers on earth that America has to explore. Purchased years ago for less than 2 cents an acre from Russia, this was thought to be a wasteland. With one of the richest oil deposits having been discovered on the north slope, it is now considered one of our prize possessions. At the present time, half of the states personal income is from government sources, and over 90 per cent of the land is government owned. Even at this, it is still a bargain.

Perhaps one of the richest natural assets in Alaska is found in Denali National Park. In Denali we have Mt. McKinley, which at 20,320 feet is the highest point in North America. In addition to the mountains, Denali is perhaps one of North America's greatest wildlife sanctuaries. While driving through Denali, it is possible to see Grizzly Bear, Moose, Caribou, or any one of a number of other wildlife species that live in protective status in this area.

Alaska also has glaciers that are easily visible from the road. Among the more prominent glaciers are Portage Glacier, which is south of Anchorage on the Seward Highway, and the Mendenhall Glacier, which is in Juneau. Various other glaciers are visible within Alaska, so be sure and ask around when you get there. On the Kenai Peninsula, Seward is an outstanding example of a commercial fishing port. While there, you might happen to see seals playing in the water, a bald eagle in the sky, or a fishing boat returning with the catch of tonights seafood.

Another feature that you will encounter that is unique to Alaska is that several of their cities are not accessible by highway. As an answer to this the State of Alaska has a very effective Marine Highway System, which is a ferry system. For a nominal charge, you and your automobile can board a ferry and go to otherwise inaccessible points by car, such as Juneau, Sitka, Wrangell, or any of the other cities on the Alaska Panhandle. Having used the ferry system, we found it to be very effective and quite satisfactory for passage to the more remote towns located along the coast.

Hawaii is perhaps one of the most unusual states that makes up the United States of America. The state is made up of seven main islands, which are Hawaii, Maui, Lanai, Molokai, Oahu, Kauai and Niihau. During the course of our visit to the islands we had the opportunity to touch on six of the seven islands. Lanai, the Pineapple Island has no tourist facilities for overnight accommodations. Niihau is called the "forbidden island" and many of the old Hawaiian ways are still existant on this island. This is a private island being used to maintain the old ways of Hawaii, and no tourist are allowed. Hawaii, the big island, is the island where the Volcano National Park is located. Oahu, is probably the second largest island, with almost 80 per cent of the state population living on it. Honolulu is located on Oahu Island. Kauai is a great place to visit with Waimea Canyon, which is Hawaii's answer to the Grand Canyon.

All of the islands are extremely pretty and with their lush vegetation, beautiful flowers, and white sand beaches. Everyone we saw seem to get the most out of every minute of everyday. Between catamarans with bright colored sails and sailboards riding over the chop off of the coast, it is truly an outdoor paradise.

All Americans should feel a special reverence for the state of Hawaii. As we recall, on December 7, 1941 a Japanese attack on the islands signaled the start of the United States involvement in World War II. With this direct attack, over 2,400 Americans lost their lives. The biggest single loss of life occurred when the U.S.S. Arizona, which was in anchorage, was hit by a 1,700 pound armor piercing bomb. In less than 9 minutes the Arizona was sunk with over 1,100 of her crew on board. With this as a memory, we feel that every American should always "Remember Pearl Harbor" and be prepared to fight in defense of this majestic nation.

California

Palm Trees are a common sight in Southern California.

Young dates hang from palm trees.

The beach near Manchester has a collection of driftwood.

The California Coast along Route 1 has ever changing scenery.

Half Dome reflects in Mirror Lake in Yosemite.

Abandoned railway bridge along entrance road to Yosemite.

An early morning mist on the edge of Kings Canyon National Park.

A rainy day in the redwoods.

Half Dome is one of the more spectacular sites in Yosemite.

Bridal Veil Falls glistens in the sunlight.

207

Half Dome, Bridal Veil Falls, and El Capitan are all visible from this viewpoint in Yosemite.

208

Oregon

Trails heighten the enjoyment of Multnomah Falls.

Scenic falls can frequently be found in eastern Oregon.

210

Scenery in the Columbia Gorge is impressive as you ride along the river.

The Bridge of the Gods joins Stevenson and Cascade Locks along the Columbia River.

Megaloose Island, originally an Indian Burial Ground.

The John Day Dam is one of many along the Columbia River.

Washington

A shadowy salmon swims upstream to spawn.

The fish viewing windows are available for visitors to observe salmon swimming upstream.

A view of the fish ladder at Rocky Reach Dam.

The Rocky Reach Dam botanist has an American Flag in flowers on the grounds.

214

The road through the Cascades gives you a closeup view of the mountains and valleys.

The ten inch disappearing guns on Whidbey Island are weapons of the past.

215

A view of the Seattle Skyline from the Ferry.

216

Alaska

General view of a valley in Denali.

A moose strolling in Denali National Park.

A view of Mt. McKinley in all it's splendor.

218

The M. V. Taku waiting to dock at Sitka.

An Indian Totem Pole stands guard at Haines, Alaska.

220

General view of ice breakup at Portage Glacier.

Rain storm along Seward Highway.

Hawaii

Sailboards enjoy the surf on Kauai.

A sailboard prepares for the challenge.

The Bird of Paradise is one of the many unusual flowers found in Hawaii.

Tropical climate and sunshine produces dense vegetation.

223

Catamaran on the Beach at Wakiki.

Wakiki Beach is tourist delight.

The Arizona Memorial stands in silent vigil of the Pearl Harbor Attack.

Akaka Falls plunges over 420 feet over a sheer drop of a volcanic cliff.

225

A beautiful sunset on the Friendly Island of Molokai.

"What America Means to Me"

Living in America means I have the option of living where I do desire. It means if I want to relocate, I can without any need for a permit. It means I can voice my opinions on whatever I so desire. It means I can be an independent businessman or I can work for a large corporation. In short, it means I can be a free man and for the most part, plot my own destiny. I have lived overseas (6 years England & 2 years in Germany) and have seen what it is like to NOT be an American. I wouldn't trade being an American; NOT FOR ANYTHING.

P.T., Port Angeles, Washington

America is a land of unlimited opportunity, freedom of speech and freedom of choice. In time of a catastrophe, the people here are ready and able to alleviate that misfortune. The flood tide of visitors and residents has been flowing into our country for a long period of time. Our land has many people who were driven from their homes and can never return. They came to American soil; we welcome them here to make their home with us. To me this is what America is all about; loving, caring and sharing to every race. I know it is the most beautiful nation in this vast world.

M.R.C., Anderson, South Carolina

This past year we had the dream of our life come true. We were able to buy an Apache Motor Home and traveled in it around the perimeter of the United States. I think if we were to sum our trip up I would say we live in a beautiful ever changing country and I am most proud to be a part of it. We left our home in Vermont on April 1st and with snow still on the ground. In the South there were flowers in bloom, prairie flowers in the desert and snow still on the mountains in the Tetons. We traveled for four months and merely had a birds eye view of this huge beautiful country. We truly hope it will be possible for us to do more traveling in the next few years because we now know there is much more for us to see in the great United States.

B. & L.P., Bennington, Vermont

When I feel overwhelmed by my surroundings, lucky just to be here, and sad for people in other countries, I am glad I am an American! The four worst things in the United States are in other countries, too . . . 1.) Rape, 2.) child-abuse, 3.)

theft, and 4.) murder. We all need to find preventions for these untolerable crimes. Our Democratic system has been and is still working on solutions. Only Americans can yell at the top of their lungs, wear any kind of clothes they want to put on in the morning, and eat any kind of food in the world. The United States gives us more choices for more people and offers more chances than any other nation. Americans should realize the privileges their ancestors have given to them and be grateful. Our country is the land of opportunity. Take yours! Life, liberty and the pursuit of happiness—what standards!!

L.W.W., Greenville, South Carolina

I am proud to be an American in that we have so much freedom to do what we like to do and can go to church and worship as we want with no conflict. It's a great place to be, thank God for America.

B.W., Anderson, South Carolina

I like America and am proud to live here. It is the best of all. We still have the Bible which I'm proud of. God's word is a light for us. In Psalms 119, Verse 5 we have these words. "Thy word is a lamp unto my feet and a light unto my path."

R.O., Pelzer, South Carolina

I am proud to be an American because Americans care. Americans believe in freedom and justice with a Democratic government by the people.

P.H., Greenville, South Carolina

I'm glad that I live in America because it is the most wonderful country in the World. I live in freedom and in love and harmony with my family and friends. I am able to worship my Lord and Savior, Jesus Christ, who died that I might live and live well. I am free to work and play and travel and to help others less fortunate than I. I am a happy American who is really thankful to be a small part of this big country.

C.S.M., Greenville, South Carolina

On a six week trip this past summer, my husband and I arrived at the Grand Canyon too late to get a campground site. A South Carolina family graciously shared their site with us and offered us some refuge from the outdoor elements, warm drinks and good conversation. We were exhausted, but exhilarated, for they had really saved the day for us by their kindness. On another occasion, upon arriving at a tiny town in northern Washington, we stopped at a restaurant for a bite to eat. A woman, noticing us crawling out of our small car, which was crammed with vacation gear and emblazoned with Michigan license plates, gave us a heartfelt greeting; "WELCOME TO WASHINGTON"! She made us feel as if we were VIP's. Those two stories show what basically friendly and giving spirits Americans are and we consider ourselves fortunate to be citizens of a country that is made up of such wonderful people.

C. & P.Mc., Big Rapids, Michigan

AMERICA

Our forefathers fought, bled and died.
Through many battles they stood side by side.
Fighting for the freedoms we have today,
With their lives, they were willing to pay.

The right to think and say what we please
is only one of these.
To cast our vote in a democratic way,
is a right we should cherish every day.

We worship openly in song and prayer,
While others around the world would not dare.
To do such a thing would cost them their life,
Would we be willing to pay this price?

America, Land of Freedom, do we realize. . . .
Our country, our nation, oh what a prize!
Unparalled beauty is here to see,
But freedom is what America means to me.

M.W.S., Greenville, S.C.

We complain so much about everything, but we're so much better off than most people. I guess the word "Freedom" stands out in my mind; freedom to make our own choices, enjoy family, friends and our country. I hope we never take the beautiful country for granted. We really are fortunate to live in America and have the freedom to enjoy it.

J.S., Burlington, Washington

229

Equipment Data

Cameras used for this book were both Leica M-4 Rangefinder Cameras (2) and Leica SL-2 MOT Single Lens Reflex Cameras (2) with Motor Drives. Lenses used were Leica 21MM to 560MM. The rangefinder was used most frequently and the single lens reflexes were used for the telephoto photography. A Metz 60CT-1 flash was used in New Orleans at the Mardi Gras Festivities.

All photographs were taken with Kodak's Kodachrome 64 transparency film and developed by Kodak Processing Laboratories. Approximately 30,000 transparencies were made and there were no camera malfunctions.